1 MONTH OF FREE READING

at
www.ForgottenBooks.com

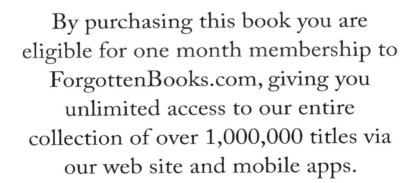

By purchasing this book you are eligible for one month membership to ForgottenBooks.com, giving you unlimited access to our entire collection of over 1,000,000 titles via our web site and mobile apps.

To claim your free month visit:
www.forgottenbooks.com/free153534

ISBN 978-0-267-21463-1
PIBN 10153534

This book is a reproduction of an important historical work. Forgotten Books uses
state-of-the-art technology to digitally reconstruct the work, preserving the original format
whilst repairing imperfections present in the aged copy. In rare cases, an imperfection in
the original, such as a blemish or missing page, may be replicated in our edition. We do,
however, repair the vast majority of imperfections successfully; any imperfections that
remain are intentionally left to preserve the state of such historical works.

A MARVELOUS HISTORY
OF MARY OF NIMMEGEN

A MARVELOUS HISTORY
OF MARY OF NIMMEGEN

PRINTED IN THE NETHERLANDS

A
MARVELOUS HISTORY OF

WHO FOR MORE *THAN* SEVE*N* YEAR
LIVED AND HAD ADO WITH THE DEVIL

———

Translated from the Middle Dutch by
HARRY MORGAN AYRES
Associate Professor in Columbia University

With an introduction by
ADRIAAN J. BARNOUW
Queen Wilhelmina Professor in Columbia University

Of this series fifty copies have been printed
on real Dutch hand-made paper, in 8vo size

INTRODUCTION

The miracle play of Mary of Nimmegen is one of the gems of Dutch mediaeval literature. Its heroine is a reincarnation of Beatrice, the runaway nun from a Brabant convent who, after wandering seven years with her paramour, and living other seven as a public woman, returned, a repentant sinner, to the convent to find that she had never been missed. For all those fourteen years the Mother of God had served, in her person, as sacristan, because Beatrice had never let a day go by without praying an Ave Maria.

The love idyll of this early legend has been turned into a grotesque caricature by the author of our miracle play. The handsome youth whose seductions proved stronger than the nun's monastic vows is changed into "an ill-favored devil of a man", as he is described by one of the tipplers in the Antwerp tavern. Leering Moonen's one eye is a mirror that distorts the smile of love into a grimace. His promise to satisfy the girl's craving for pleasure and finery is the substitute magic whereby he works his charm upon her, and even that would have failed of its effect without the aid of Mary's fit of despair. Despondency is the devil's abettor. To us moderns, accustomed to the searching analysis of mental reactions, the girl's easy surrender to both the fit and the fiend is not sufficiently accounted for. But the author of "Mary of Nimmegen" did not attempt to unravel the involutions of the mind. His aim was to glorify the ways of God's mother to man, and the actions of man required no further exposition than sufficed to exemplify her divine mercy in its fullness. For that purpose the relation between cause and effect could be expressed in the simplest of terms, such as give force to the proverbial wisdom of those early days. Wanhope is the devil's snare. That homely truth, a reflection of the mediaeval doctrine that wanhope was one of the sins against the Holy Ghost, is illustrated by Mary's reckless invocation of "either God or all the fiends of Hell", and Moonen appears on the scene at once in accordance with the Dutch adage which says that when you speak of the devil you tread on his tail. English sense of decorum, which shuns the mention of the unspeakable one, pretends to hear the flutter of wings when it speaks of an angel of heaven. Dutch love of realism, in scorning to barter the tangible tail under foot for the invisible wings over head, is truer to the experience of life, for weak humanity has always been more easily susceptible to the suggestive power of evil than of good.

Mary of Nimmegen finds it so. Her "God or the Devil, 't is all one to me", is a vain pretence at impartial allegiance. Who stands at the parting of the ways to Heaven and Hell, waiting for God to call or for the Devil to snatch her, has already passed beyond the point of retrievement. The response to the divine summons will require a moral effort which the snatcher will spare her. The way of least resistance is the way to Hell.

Mary is never in doubt as to the real nature of her one-eyed companion. "Ye be the devil out of hell!", is her reply to Moonen's introduction of himself and in her first lament over the sinful life she is leading she admits to her own soul that

> "Though he saith little, I may not him mistake:
> He is a fiend or but little more."

The innocent maiden who lived a blameless life in her uncle's home has, by one night's experience, become a hardened sinner. It is difficult for a modern reader to believe in Mary's sudden wickedness. But we must remember that the mediaeval playwright did not mean to show his audience the consecutive stages of her degradation. The action on the stage is an epitome of that mental process, condensing temptation and surrender into one simple scene, the intervening phases of mental struggle and agony being left to the imagination of the audience. The language, which is more conservative than the stage, has retained that simple allegory which modern drama has discarded: we still speak of "a fallen girl", although we demand from the modern playwright that he show us how she slid into sin.

While the inner life is thus translated into the

simplest of allegories, life's visible pageant is mirrored in all its variety. Its realistic portrayal is the chief beauty of this drama. In the romantic playlets of "Esmoreit" and of "Lanseloot" a faint reflection is seen of courtly manners imported from France. In "Mary of Nimmegen" the everyday life of Netherlands burghers is astir on the stage. We get a glimpse of the simple household of a village priest, who, not unknown to his niece, dabbles in necromancy, we are introduced into the low life of Antwerp and hear the drawer's call to the tapster repeating an order, "A first, ho, a first! Draw of the best and fill to the brim!", we watch with the good people of Nimmegen the performance of a mystery on a pageant-wain in the market-place, and see women take a passionate part in the political factions of the day.

This participation of women in politics was evidently characteristic of the Netherlands. Their meddling with affairs of state suggested to an English dramatist of a later period a vivid scene between an English gentlewoman and a group of Dutch Pankhursts. They counsel her to follow their example:

> "You are wellcom, Lady
> And your comming over hether is most happy :
> For here you may behold the generall freedom
> We live and traffique in, the ioy of woemen.
> No emperious Spanish eye governes our actions,
> Nor Italian jealouzie locks up our meetings:
> We are ourselves our owne disposers, masters;
> And those that you call husbands are our Servants.
> . . . .
>   Do you think there's any thing
> Our husbands labour for, and not for our ends ?
> Are we shut out of Counsailes, privacies,
> And onely lymitted our household business?
> No, certaine, Lady, we pertake with all,
> Or our good men pertake no rest." [1]

1 *The Tragedy of Sir John van Olden Barnavelt (1619).*

Women in the Netherlands were evidently emancipated before their sisters elsewhere. The Italian Quirini, Venetian envoy to the Court at Brussels, in the early sixteenth century, was amazed at the freedom the women of Antwerp enjoyed. "The ladies", he wrote in 1506, "wear bright costumes and spend all their leisure, when the work is done, in dancing, singing, and playing musical instruments, giving themselves entirely over to pleasure. They keep house, in addition, and manage all domestic affairs, without their husbands' control." And when Albrecht Dürer visited Antwerp, with his wife and maid, in the autumn of 1520, he found it difficult to bring his own ideas of decorum into line with the equality which there prevailed between the sexes. At the banquet given in his honor by the Guild of St. Luke, the artists' wives were all present, and

Dürer could not do otherwise than bring his women companions to the feast. But at his inn in the Wool-street where he could live in German fashion, he let his wife and maid have their meals in the kitchen, and took his own in the parlor with mine host.

The Antwerp that Dürer knew can not have been much different from that where Moonen and Mary lived for seven years. For hardly more than a generation had passed, in 1520, since the author conceived his play. The wicked aunt's fealty to Duke Adolf of Guelders is a motif extraneous to the plot, as poetic justice demands that her suicide be an atonement for her cruelty to young Mary, but it reconciles the historian to its preposterous intrusion by affording him a clue to the date of composition of the drama. The old Duke Aernout was imprisoned by his son in the year 1465, and in 1471 occurred his release,

which stirred the virago's wrath to such a pitch that
"she cut her throat out of pure spite". At the time
of Mary and Moonen's return to Nimmegen three
years had gone by since her death, and Mary, after
her pilgrimage to Rome, is said in the Epilogue to
have survived the miracle of the rings for "about
two years." The play does not tell us how many
years her penance lasted, but supposing that it was
short and that the author wrote soon after Mary's
death, the date of composition can hardly have been
much earlier than 1480. It matters little whether the
poet dramatized historical events or an invented story.
The records of the town of Nimmegen contain no
reference to a performance of the wain-pageant of
Maskeroon, nor has a trace been found of Mary's
grave, with the three rings suspended over it, in the
convent for converted sinners at Maastricht. But

even if she were a fictitious character, the author, while inserting these chronological data into the play, imagined the incidents of his female rake's progress as actual occurrences in a recent past, which justifies the historian's use of these data in trying to fix the date of composition.

If the poet were also the writer of the prose sections, it would be wrong to ignore the statement that Mary's uncle, after their visit to the Pope, lived yet, according to the earliest version, for twenty-four years in his village near Nimmegen. The author recording events of a quarter of a century ago would, in that case, have written, at the earliest, in the year 1498. But there is good ground to believe that the poet was not responsible for the interpolated prose, which is not essential to the play on the stage. Some Dutch critics hold the prose to be part of the drama as originally written, and intended to be spoken by a stage manager who supplied in his narrative the missing links between the scenes. But the fact is that only in a few instances does the prose serve that purpose, and in those isolated cases the imagination of the audience could be relied upon to help itself By far the greater part of the prose narrative either repeats the drift of the preceding dialogue or anticipates the incidents of later scenes. The first meeting between Mary and her aunt is introduced by a short account in prose from which we gather that the aunt "held of the side of the young Duke, and after did destroy herself whenas she learned that the old Duke was made quit of prison". If this was destined to be addressed to the audience from the stage, not the past, but the present, tense would have been in order. But apart from this grammatical unfitness for a speaker's rôle, these words are dramatically unfit as they forestall the surprise of the audience at the aunt's scornful reception of her niece. That the author can not be guilty of thus crudely spoiling his own creation is sufficiently evident from many instances of his insight into the exigencies of dramatic technique. By premonition and foreboding he will give the audience an inkling of imminent calamity, but to blurt out the full truth before the truth is seen in action is not his manner. When Mary has departed from her uncle, the good priest becomes aware of a heaviness that he can not explain:

> "Scarce had the maiden from me gone,
> It came o'er my spirits, how I can not tell.
> I fear with her or me 'twill not go well."

The audience get an intimation that something awful is impending, but they are kept in suspense as to what it will be and who will be the victim, whether Mary or her uncle. In that we observe the subtle touch of the artist who wrote the dialogue. He can not have been the same man who inserted the superfluous and meddlesome prose.

How, then, must we account for its intrusion if the prose did not originally form part of the play? The manner in which the drama has been preserved accounts for it. "Mary of Nimmegen" has not come down to us in manuscript form. The earliest known version is a printed chapbook from the press of Willem Vorsterman of Antwerp, who was admitted as a member of St. Luke's Guild in 1512, and remained at work in that city until 1543. The volume is not dated but probably came from the press in 1518 or 1519. Printed plays were a novelty at that early date. Vorsterman may have felt that to publish a drama *in* book *form needed some justification. The word that was intended to be spoken could not be made to serve the reader's purpose without a compromise between the dramatic and the epic. For the book is the story-teller's domain, and the dialogue was not felt to be a story until the narrator's "quoth he" subordinated every speech to his control. That seems to be the purpose of the inserted prose sections. They were not written, in the first instance, to elucidate situations left indistinct by the dramatist, but to lend to the drama the semblance of a narrative and thereby justify its appearance in print. Willem Vorsterman was careful not to offer his book to the public as a play: "A very marvelous story of Mary of Nimmegen who for more than seven years lived and had ado with the devil", is his description of the contents of the volume on its title-page. And the* three subsequent editions, that of 1608 by Herman van Borculo, of Utrecht, that of 1615 by Pauwels Stroobant, of Antwerp, and a reprint of the latter probably published in Holland, though falsely bearing the imprint of Stroobant on the title-page, all persist in calling the book a "story", be it a "very marvelous" according to Vorsterman, or a "beautiful and very marvelous and true" according to Van Borculo and Stroobant. The printers knew too well that the play's dramatic qualities would not secure its ready sale. The moral tale it embodied, not its literary form, was its chief attraction, and as a "story" it made its appeal to the reading public.

This popular estimate of the drama as literature accounts for the manner in which an English translator of "Mary of Nimmegen" felt free to handle the original. "Here begynneth a lyttell story that was of a trwethe done in the lande of Gelders of a mayde that was named Mary of Nemmegen that was the dyuels paramoure by the space of vij yere longe", runs the title of this rendering, and its "Amen" is followed by the statement, "Thus endeth this lyttell treatyse Imprynted at Anwarpe by me John Duisbrowghe dwellynge besyde the camer porte." The story in dialogue as printed by Vorsterman became a "treatyse" in the English version as printed, in probably the same year, by his fellow citizen Jan van Doesborch. Vorsterman left the dialogue of the playwright intact from no scrupulous respect for an author's work of art. It suited his convenience to print it as it was written, his own prose, or that of the scribbler he employed, being sufficient to justify his labeling the book a "story". But the translator, who had to re-word the entire dialogue in any case, had no reasons of convenience to make him spare the poet's creation. He made a fairly literal rendering of the interpolated prose and turned the dramatic dialogue into a clumsily phrased narrative, of which the following extract may serve as a sample:

> "When they were come to Nemmegyn it fortuned on the same that it was the dilycacyon of a chyrche, and when they were within the Towne than sayde Emmekyn to Satan let us goo see howe my aunte dothe, than sayde Satan ye nede nat go to hyr for she is dead more than a yere a goo, than sayd Emmekyn is it trewth, than sayd Satan ye, than sayd Emmekyn to the dyuell what do all yender folks that be yender gathered than sayde the dyuell the play a play that is wont every yere to be played, than sayde Emmekyn good love let us goo here it for I have harde my vnckyll say often tymes that a play were better than a sermant to some folke."

The Englishman who perpetrated this murder of a good book was not more guilty in intention than

Willem Vorsterman, only the result of his labor, due to the different task he undertook, makes him seem the greater sinner of the two.

Although extraneous to the play as it was acted, the prose is not altogether a negligible accretion. For its writer evidently drew on his recollections of the play as he had seen it staged for his description of some of the incidents. The quarrel between the aunt and her gossips, enacted by their shouting and cursing and pulling of each other's hair; the row stirred up by Moonen among the crowd that listened to Mary's recital of a "goodly ballat", one among the folk being stabbed to death, whereupon "he who did this had his head smote off"; the manslaughter committed by one of Mary's potmates at the Golden Tree; the uncle locking the rings round Mary's neck and hands; these are apparently bits of pantomime as essentially part of the play as is the written context. And because of its value as the only testimony we possess of an eye-witness of the drama's production on the mediaeval stage, the prose has been retained by the present translator, his book being a faithful reproduction in English of the earliest version of the play as printed by Willem Vorsterman.

Of the author of our little drama nothing is known. He was, doubtless, not a native of the good town of Nimmegen. For it appears from verse 652 that he imagined Mary's uncle to live at Venlo, and a citizen of Nimmegen would have known that the distance between these two places was not a three hours' walk but four times as long. The poet was evidently more familiar with the city of Antwerp, and his picture of the drinking scene in the tavern of the Golden Tree is vivid enough to be a first-hand impression. He was a poet of no mean talent, and not unconscious, it seems, of his own excellence in the noble art of rhetoric. The pride of the poets of the Renaissance is forestalled in his praise of poesy, of which he made *Mary* his mouthpiece:

> "Rhetoric is not to be learned by skill.
> 'Tis an art that cometh of itself solely.
> The other arts, if a man giveth himself thereto wholly,
> These be to be learned and eke taught.
> But rhetoric is to be praised beyond aught.
> 'Tis a gift of the Holy Ghost's bestowing."

The goodly ballat lamenting in its refrain that "through folly falls poesy to decay" seems itself to bear the marks of folly's blight. It was a concession to the taste of the day, which held the accumulation of rhymes, the use of grandiloquent gallicisms, and the elaborate structure of stanzas — all skilfully reproduced in Mr. Ayres' rendering — to be the elements of poetry. That was the kind of versification admired and cultivated in the so-called Chambers of Rhetoric, a kind of mediaeval theatre guilds where the local poets and poetasters imbibed the love of poetry with their beer. But our author, who believed in "Poeta nascitur, non fit", proved by his own achievement that neither can the born poet be unmade by the temporary vagaries of poetic fashion. Where he wrote the language that his mother had taught him, instead of the bombast admired among the brethren of his craft, it yielded true poetry, vibrant with emotion in the lyrical parts, and full of plastic force in its realistic passages. Intricate rhyme schemes are employed to emphasize the lyrical note, but the verse runs on so smoothly through the reverberation of sounds, and the language remains so simple and direct, that the artificial effort does not obtrude itself upon our notice. Sometimes the dialogue assumes the form of a rondeau, and in the scene between uncle and aunt this device is applied with consummate skill, the uncle's sad lament "Alas, my sister, ye deceive me", which is its "leitmotif", becoming intensified at its second and third repetition by its contrast with the aunt's replies, which proceed from mockery at her clodpate brother John to heartless slander of the lost girl. The poet's device of varying the rhyme scheme of the dialogue according to the mood of the speakers has been carefully reproduced by the translator, so that the reader can form his own opinion of its effectiveness.

Apart from its poetical qualities the play of "Mary of Nimmegen" deserves to be read—and enacted, to be sure—because it is a fine specimen of mediaeval drama. Recent productions in Holland have shown *that the play does not miss its effect upon a twentieth-century audience. The author selected a plot which yielded to modern literature two of its noblest dramatic compositions. For the heroine of the Dutch poet is a female prototype of Faust and of Tannhäuser. To have been the first to discover its fitness for the stage is a title of distinction for our playwright, and we regret our ignorance that can not link his name, as it deserves, with those greater names of Marlowe, Goethe and Wagner. His drama also affords an early instance of the effective introduction of the play within the play. It served a double purpose in this case. For not only did the show of "Maskeroon" cause Mary to repent her sinful life, but it was, at the same time, an "oratio pro domo" of the poet, as it fitly impressed the audience with the ethical value of his art. "Better than many a preaching," was the*

village priest's verdict. And we, of the twentieth century, can agree with him, though we do not share the
poet's Mariolatry. For Heaven's joy over a repentant
sinner must ever find its echo in the poetry of this
world which is a gift of Heaven to its chosen. And
of those chosen was our nameless author. The play
of "Maskeroon" has long ceased to impress repentant
Maries, but „Mary of Nimmegen" herself has at-
tained immortality, thanks to her maker's gift, which
was of the Holy Ghost's bestowing.

PROLOGUE

n the days that Duke Arent of Guelders was done in
prison at Grave by his son Duke Adolf and his knav-
ish fellows there dwelt three mile from Nimmegen
a devout priest hight Sir Gysbrecht, and with him
dwelt a fair young maid hight Mary, his sister's
daughter, whose mother was dead. And this aforesaid
maid kept her uncle's house serving him in all needful with honesty and diligence.

❡ How Sir Gysbrecht hath sent his niece Mary to
Nimmegen.

It chanced that this Sir Gysbrecht would send his
niece Mary to Nimmegen there to buy what so they
needed, saying to her thus:

Mary!

MARY

What would ye, my good eme?

UNCLE

Hark, child, give heed as doth beseem.
Get ye to Nimmegen with all speed
To fetch straight our provisions; we have need
Of candles, of oil in the lamp to set;
Salt, vinegar, and onions eke must ye get,
And store of sulphur matches, as ye say truly.
Here be eight stivers, go hen and buy
In Nimmegen what so we lack, as ye well may.
It is by good hap the week's market day,
So shall ye the better find what ye desire.

MARY

Good eme, to do even as ye require
Ye know me ready; I will go my gait.

UNCLE

This even to win home again if it be too late,
For the days be now full short the while,
And 'tis hither to Nimmegen two great mile,

And now ten o' the clock, or well more,
Heark, child, and if ye may not give o'er
Ere by broad day, as it seemeth you,
Ye may win home as ye would fain do,
Bide there the night, I would be the more at ease,
And go sleep at thine aunt's, my sister, if it please;
She will not deny you for a night but one.
I had liefer that, than ye should over stile and stone
Come homewards darkling and alone all wholly;
For the road is of stout knaves none too free.
And ye be a maid, but young and fair thereto,
And like to be accosted.

MARY

Eme, as it pleaseth you,
I will nought other do than as ye tell.

UNCLE

Greet me your aunt, my sister, and farewell.
Buy what we lack by weight and measure true.

MARY

I will, good eme; adieu.

UNCLE

Dear niece, adieu.

God's grace be ever thy company. —

Lord God, why doth my heart so heavy lie?
Is it that the land so sorely is distraught?
Or that my niece may in some snare be caught?
Stay, whence this heaviness? 'T is strange to think upon.
Scarce had the maiden from me gone
It came o'er my spirits, how I cannot tell.
I fear with her or me 't will not go well.
Would I had kept her with me at home.
'Tis madness at their will to let roam
Young maids or women through the countryside.
The knavery of this world is deep and wide.

¶ How Mary was shamefully bespoken of her aunt.

Thus is Mary departed from her uncle and come
unto Nimmegen, where she did buy all that was
needful for her or her uncle. And on the selfsame
day that she was come to Nimmegen her aunt had
fallen out with four or five of her gossips concerning
the Duke Adolf who had done into prison the old

Duke his father. So that she was the rather mad or a
raging she-devil than a Christian wight; for she held
of the side of the young Duke, and after did destroy
herself whenas she learned that the old Duke was
made quit of prison by the hand of the chastelain of
Grave, as ye will hereafter learn. Mary, seeing that
it grew to evening when she had done all those
things for the which she had come to Nimmegen,
said unto herself thus:

Now have I all such as we wanted,
By weight and measure no whit scanted,
Bought and duly therefor paid.
But meseems I have here so long delayed
That yonder is the night risen well nigh.
There is a dial, whereon I may espie
The hour of the day. 'Tis already betwixt four and five.
Here I must get me a lodging, as I would thrive.
There remains yet an hour more of day,
And in three hours I scarcely may
Win home to mine eme's. Nay, to stay here were best.
Mine aunt dwelleth hard by, as I have guessed.
I will go pray her that she make me a bed,

An on the morrow, so soon as I be awak'ned,
I will haste me home to my task once more.
I see mine aunt standing before her door.
In seemly wise I will her greet. —
Aunt, may Christ make all your sorrow sweet,
And all them you love keep both fair and well.

AUNT

Fy, welcome, devil, how do ye in hell?
Well, mistress, what would ye hereabout?

MARY

Mine eme sent me at noon, without a doubt,
For candles, mustard, vinegar and verjuice
And for such other as at home we have use;
And ere I could run from one thing to another in hie
And search out each and all and then buy,
It is grown so late; and little may it misease you
That as for tonight ye make me a bed, an it please you.
I would e'en now get me home, but in the night
There be those who lie in wait for maids to do them des-
Ay, and dishonor, so that they have shame of it; [pite,
And for that I am afraid.

AUNT

Out upon it, chit!
God a mercy! Make ye so much pother about a maiden-
Fy, dear niece, ye ken well how ye were bred   [head?
This long time, though ye pretend to such dismay.
Nor with your household matters since noonday
Ye have not been busy, as to my thinking.

MARY

In good sooth, aunt, I have.

AUNT

Yea, or sitting a-drinking
In some snug corner with "fill the can, fill."
Fy, niece, in the country Dickon or Will
Know well how to go with the lasses amids the rye,
And when at even their sports they ply,
Hath not Gill won a pretty forfeit from Jack?
Fy, niece, ere now ye have got a green gown to your
At home, I doubt not, many brisk lads there be. [back.

MARY

Why say ye so, aunt?

AUNT

                 Ay, mistress hypocrisy!
Though the truth on't cannot be told, I'll be bound,
Ye have tripped it lightly many a round
Where the piper got not five groats for his noise.
Let 'em go to it never so with the boys,
'Tis all virgin, ay, till girdles be let out.

MARY

That I should be so shent and shamed, without
All guilt, is more than heart can bear.

AUNT

And I have spoke with them too who would swear
They saw you and your own eme in such guise
That it cannot be told of in no seemly wise.
All our kin ye bring to scandal and shame.
Tush, vile progeny, ye be too much to blame,
Out of my sight! Ye do mine eyes no good!

MARY

Lord God, what woe is mine in mood!
How doth the blood forsake my body utterly.
So vile reproach, such words of ignomy,

8

To hear and suffer, all unmerited!
Now, aunt, tell me if ye will make me a bed
For this one night?

AUNT

> Ye were me liefer lie,

As deep as this roof-tree is high,
In the Meuse as bait for all its fish.
Be gone, ere you repent your wish.
I tremble like a leaf for teen.

MARY

Ye do me wrong, aunt.

AUNT

> Stay, this cursed quean

With vexing me will not be done or quit.
Would ye have those fine braids tousled a bit? —
Yea, she rouses the maggot in my head.
I could bring the devil himself to bed
And bind him to the pillow like a doting wight.
I be grown so awry with spite,
I know not if I stand on head or feet.
To them withall that I today meet

I shall make answer, wherefor wrathful I am,
Even the same answer as the devil giveth his dam.

MARY

Ah, wretch! now be ye fallen on sorry days.
I stand here as one in a maze,
And of myself I know not the what or the how;
Meseems, I should have run frantic from the town
Mindful nor of knaves nor of thieves.   [erenow,
Under the trees I will make me a bed of leaves.
I reck not whom I meet, be it fremd or kin,
Though the devil came in his own proper skin.
To ask no questions thinketh me best.
Under this hedge I will sit me down to rest,
Yielding myself, for ill or well,
To god or all the fiends of hell.

⁋ How Mary took leave of her aunt and departed
out of Nimmegen.

Thus is the young maiden, Mary, departed from her
aunt and piteously weeping in sore distress hath
betaken her out of the town Nimmegen in the dark
of evening, until she is come to a great thick hedge,

beneath the which she sat her down in sorrowful mood, weeping and wailing, and oft commending herself to the devil, and to herself sorrowfully saying:

Weeping and wailing and mine hands wringing,
Calling myself maledight,
Be all my solace and none other thing,
By cause mine aunt hath done me despite.
Is it wrong that I should be in spite
That causeless she blaméd me at erst?
Nay! Such anger doth on me alight
And waxeth in my heart aright,
That I sit here in wrathful plight
And ever hold myself accurst.

Help, what temptations on me throng!
Shall I yet do some violence?
Ah, youth, canst thou bear up so long?
Can reason offer no defence?
How should I stomach such offence
All guiltless? Whosoe'er he be,
None living hath patience.
Wanhope doth drive me from my sense.

11

Help me lament mine innocence,
God or the Devil, 't is all one to me.

¶ The Devil, who always spreadeth his nets and
snares wherein to catch souls ripe unto damnation,
on hearing these words said with himself as follows:

Ah! I'm the richer by one more soul!
Ye see me disguised and, on the whole,
Quite the sort of gentleman God approves,
And, except for my one eye, just as behoves;
The other perchance was cast out by a spell.
It's not in our power, we devils of hell,
To incarnate ourselves, as ye are aware,
Without some little defect here or there,
Be it in the head or the hands or the feet.
Now as I may I will make my voice sweet,
And speak with such modest and winsome cheer
As to do none offense to my sweet lemman here.
With the women 'tis doucely at first that gets on.
Fair child, why sit ye here sorrow-begone?
Hath some one misdone you, sans reason or right,
As a good honest fellow would gladly requite?

12

The picture of innocence, child, ye resemble,
Wherefore I would comfort you.

MARY

       Help, God, how I tremble!
How stands it with me? I know not aright
Since first this good man came on my sight.
Help, how all faintly throbbeth my heart!

THE DEVIL

Fair child, fear ye no grief nor smart.
I will do you neither harm nor let,
But I make avouch if your course ye will set
By my avise, and go with me by all means,
I will make you ere long a queen among queens.

. . . .

MARY

       . . . . . Friend,
I sit now all at my wits' end,
This my machine so wrought to hurt
By shameful words, the which without desert
I needs must bear: slut, harlot, whore,
That to the Fiend I'd liefly give me o'er
As to God, for I be half from my wit.

13

THE DEVIL

By Lucifer, 'tis purchase, all of it!
She hath drunk up her wrath at one
And sits in wanhope like a stone.
Hope bids me shed no tears today:
I shall not fail. — Fair child, I pray
That we in friendship may agree.

MARY

Who are ye, friend?

THE DEVIL

A master of much subtlety,
Who never comes short in aught he essays.

MARY

It skills not with whom I go my ways,
As well with the worst as with the best.

THE DEVIL

If to mewards your love were dress'd
I would teach you in all their parts
Music, rhetoric, all the seven arts,
Logic, grammar, geometry,
Arithmetic and alchemy,

14

All the which be worthy of heed;
No woman on earth in learning shall speed
As ye shall do.

MARY

       Ye should have potent gramerye.
Who may ye be?

THE DEVIL

           Why, what care ye?
To ask me that 'twere wiser not.
In truth, I am not the best of my lot.
But none could love you as well as I.

MARY

How hight ye, friend?

THE DEVIL

       Moonen with the single eye,
Whom all good fellows know right well.

MARY

Ye be the devil out of hell!

THE DEVIL

At least your humble servant and true friend.

MARY

Strange, but ye do not me offend.
Though Lucifer self were come from hell,
I stand in case to greet him well.
I be wholly quit of fear.

THE DEVIL

So this is the short and long, my dear:
If you will do after my rate,
All that your fancy may dictate
I'll teach you, as at erst I told.
Of goods, of jewels, or of gold
Ye shall never more have need,

MARY

Tis well said; but by your rede,
Ere we be given each to each,
The seven arts ye shall me teach,
For in such learning I would speed.
Ye will me teach them?

THE DEVIL

Faith, in deed.

All seemly lore I will impart.

MARY

Nigromancy is a merry art.
Mine eme therein hath a pretty wit.
He hath a book and wonders works with it,
Nor never fails, he is so sly.
He can through the needle's eye
Send the devil a-creeping willy-nilly.
That trick I fain would learn.

THE DEVIL

Ah, silly,

My knowledge is wholly at your device.
But I never studied, to be precise,
Nigromancy in all its parts.
It is quite the hardest of all the arts,
And for a novice perilous as well.
Suppose there's wanting in your spell
A word or letter wherewithal
Ye would make the spirit that ye call
Your wishes duly to obey,
The fiend would break your neck straightway.
My dear, be sure there's mischief in it.

17

MARY

Well, in that case I'll not begin it.
I would not meet death in such a kind.

THE DEVIL

Ha, ha! I've put that out of her mind,
What would she be wanting to learn such a thing?
An she did, it would not be long ere she'd bring
On all us poor spirits the worst of our fears,
At her own sweet will set all hell by the ears,
And force even me in some dreadful tight squeak.
I teach her nigromancy? Not this week!
It is something at all costs she must not consider of. —
Now hearken to what I shall teach you, my love.
If nigromancy ye will wholly let be.

MARY

What will ye teach me?

THE DEVIL

Ah, let us see.

I will make you master of every tongue,
So that far and wide your fame shall be rung.

18

In the knowledge of tongues much virtue abides,
And the seven liberal arts there besides.
Ye shall be exalted of all and each.

MARY

My sorrow wanes at your fair speech.
Do that, and wholly at your will
I hold me.

THE DEVIL

       One little matter still;
But grant my prayer, and well will you betide.

MARY

What is your prayer?

THE DEVIL

      To lay your name aside.
And give yourself another therefor.
Mary's a name I never learned to care for.
Along of one Mary I and my fellows into such mischief
That 'tis a name we like but indifferent well. [fell
Were ye called Lisbeth or Lina or Gretchen, my dear,
It would get you more, I'll be sworn, in a year
Than ever ye had of kin or kith.

MARY

Alas, wherefore do ye take ill therewith?
'Tis ever the sweetest and noblest name
That the tongue of man can fashion or frame.
Why should ye thereagainst make war?
I may not change, for worlds and more,
A name which nought could make more sweet.

THE DEVIL

Tut, tut! It's all about one's feet
Again, but if she will thereto consent! —
Would we, my dear, to our content
Go wandering, ye must change that name,
Or here we part. Yet more I claim
Of you. A promise is a debt.

MARY

What must it be?

THE DEVIL

Not to forget,
Come weal, come woe, I cannot bear
To have you cross yourself.

20

MARY

I grant it well and fair.
On crossing I set but little store.
But my name I can ill brook to give o'er.
For Maria, whence I have it, is my hope and trust,
And when in sorrow I am thrust
I cry on her to intercede.
Daily thus I bid my bede
Even as a child I learned it of yore.
Praised be Mary evermore!
While I have life I will ne'er have done,
Though wild and wanton I may run,
With praising her, nor at all forget.

THE DEVIL

Well, since your will be wholly set
Upon this name, I will somewhat abate:
Of all the letters keep at any rate
The first and drop the other three;
That is the M, and Emma shall ye be,
As in your countryside be many a maid and dame.

MARY

Well, since I may not have my proper name

I were indeed to blame, if we parted for a letter;
Emma I am, since I may be no better :
But still I like it not.

THE DEVIL

Nay, come,
If ye have not everything beneath your thumb
Within the year, I have nought to say.
Haste we to Bolduc without a stay
And thenceward let us take no rest
Ere to Antwerp we have pressed ;
There we shall a wonder show.
By that, the tongues ye shall wholly know
At your desire, I pledge me to 't,
And the seven liberal arts, to boot.
Bastard and malmsey shall ye drink.
But be my friend and ye may not think
Of the marvels all ye shall do and see. —
But at last your soul belongs to me !

After these words Emma and Moonen have taken
their way to Bolduc, where for some while they

tarried, feasting merrily, and paying the shot of each
and all who ate and drank in their company.

Now shall we stint a little of Emma and Moonen
and tell of Sir Gysbrecht, her eme.

After that Mary, the which now hight Emma, had
been for some while away, Sir Gysbrecht, her eme,
much wondered at her tarrying, and said with himself thus:

O anxiety, which clamors within me strong,
How dost thou rend my heart and my wit molest.
For that my niece Mary doth bide so long
Who to Nimmegen market hath her dress'd,
Where if it grew dark, I told her, as for the best,
Or haply in any wise she were frighted,
She should at my sister's seek her rest;
There ever I lodge when I am benighted.
Nor will my troubled heart be righted
Ere I know how she doth speed.
If mischief on her hath alighted,
I die without all hope or rede,
For the lass is all I have at need,
And ever from childhood hath been my care;

If foul befall her 'twere woe indeed.
These lasses lightly fall in despair.
Now to Nimmegen I repair
To get me tidings without fail.
Men oft must hear a sorry tale.

After these words is Sir Gysbrecht gone to his sister's house, asking after Mary, the niece of them both, the which answered rudely that she wist nought of her. Whereat he was right sad, saying to her thus:

Alas, my sister, ye deceive me,
When ye say that of Mary ye nothing wot.

AUNT

Nay, good clodpate John, believe me.

UNCLE

Alas, my sister, ye deceive me.

AUNT

Nay, she is cloistered, I conceive me
Where such birds be spitted for a groat.

UNCLE

Alas, my sister, ye deceive me,
When ye say that of her ye nothing wot;

24

And thus with wrath yourself besot,
Though I bid you but tell in all gentleness
If ye have seen her.

AUNT

Natheless,

Say ye not her charge was mine.
She came, 'tis true, eight or ten days syne,
Saying, "Make me a bed, aunt, for to-night
I dare not go home, lest I be done despight
Of knaves who would lightly some mischief begin."
I bade her take her once more to the inn
Where the livelong day she had sat drinking and
[skinking.

UNCLE

How! had she the livelong day been a-drinking?

AUNT

That you may well be thinking, and nothing loath.
And her cheeks were as red, I make an oath,
As a baby's bottom that has been well thwack'd.
When I blamed her a little for her shameful fact,

She made as with good sharp sauce she could eat me
Thus cursing and shouting she goes her gate, [straight.
And no more of my fine young lady I see.

UNCLE

Alas, what shall become of me?
O God in three, where hath she gone or far or near?

AUNT

Why, goodman dull, in the muddy wine or clear,
Where they resort as for such sport are meet.

UNCLE

Alas, my sister, ye gar me greet,
That ye make me such shameful mocks.

AUNT

Yea, had ye kept her locked up in a box,
So had your trouble not begun.
God's son, goodman, what harm is done
If she follow her lust at large a bit?
It will not matter to her no whit
Nor fare the worse by a single straw.
She will not go halt for it.

UNCLE

This doth my spirit so adaw
I fear mine heart in four will cleave.
I must turn me about and with my sleeve
Wipe from mine eyes and cheeks a tear.

O mother of God, the which each year
In Aix I visit and adore,
Help me now as ye have done yore,
And ye in Maestricht, Saint Servace,
Devoutly have I set in place
Full many a candle, as ye wot:
I pray you now, forsake me not.

In time of need it is to one's friends one must look;
I will now let search for her in every nook
If any of her may have heard.
Though I be stirred,
'Tis but small wonder that I grieve :
Of lief 'tis ill to take one's leave.

After this Sir Gysbrecht departed him from his sister
sad at heart because he gat no tidings of Mary his
niece.

27

❡ How the wicked aunt thrust a dagger in her throat.

In the meanwhile the chastelain of Grave let the old duke Arent forth of the prison and led him to the town of Bolduc where he was right royally received by the lords of that same. Which hearing, the wicked aunt waxed so wrathful in her venomous heart that she well nigh burst for spite, saying:

Help me, liver, lights, and spleen,
Teeth and head, nought goes aright!
I shall smother or split with teen:
Like a spider I swell with spite;
From my wits I be thrust out quite
At the tidings that I hear.
The old thief, in the castle that was locked tight,
He is got from Grave scot-free and clear.
Now all my comfort is but drear,
And the young duke, whom I obeyed,
Will shortly have but sorry cheer.
Such woe is me that I am near
To yield me, body and soul as I was made,
And summon all devils to mine aid.

THE DEVIL

Ha, ha! there's profit as in this case!
Her soul is mine if I have the space
Of half an hour on her to bestow.

AUNT

Is it not noyous?

THE DEVIL

                Yea, and a shrewd blow
To them as were counted the young duke's men.

AUNT

To say the truth on't, what is he, then,
Who ever a finer fellow saw with eye?
Yea, though in hell I must everlastingly fry,
I could cut my throat out of pure spite,
So I were done with this business quite.
Adieu and farewell, valiant young peer.
But so ye be duke in after year
Is all I ask for my shortened life.
Thus in my throat I thrust the knife
And with a blow I end me quite.
Faction has damned full many a wight.

THE DEVIL

To Hell's convocation, in unending dole,
I summon this soul to its final fruition.
The folly of men who in factions enroll
And for some princeling get damned to perdition!
They are ours! all ours, who in this condition
Persist stubborn-hearted despite of all ill.
Envious faction gives yearly addition
To Hell of its millions, lament it who will.

❡ How Emma and Moonen journeyed to Antwerp,
where they wrought much evil.

When Emma and Moonen had for some while tarried at Bolduc they journeyed to Antwerp whither
they be speedily come. And Moonen said unto Emma
thus:

Now be we in Antwerp, as ye well would,
Here will we triumph and scatter our good.
Go we in to the "Tree" for a pint of romany.

EMMA

To the "Tree", say ye?

30

MOONEN

Yes, faith, there shall ye see
All the spendthrifts that thrive by mischance;
And the wenches who know well all the old dance,
The which on ten and four hazard all at a throw.
Above sit the burghers, and the craft below,
With whom 'tis more blessed to take than to give.

EMMA

All that I would liefly behold, as I live.
Nought could be better, as to my thinking.

MOONEN

Yea, in the Gold Room we shall be drinking
Ere that we part what pleaseth you most.
Sit down, love. Yea, a first, mine host!
And if it grew musty in cask, we were evil paid.

THE DRAWER

What wine drink ye, good man?

MOONEN

A pint of grenade,
And for my wife a pint of ypocras,

And of romany a pint, the which nought doth surpass
To raise a man's spirits when they be low.

THE DRAWER

Ay, that's the truth. A first! ho! a first! ho!
Draw of the best and fill to the brim!

FIRST TIPPLER

See, Hans, yon is a wench that is trim.

SECOND TIPPLER

Ye say sooth, and but an ill-favored devil of a man!

FIRST TIPPLER

Let us sit by them and drink of our can.
If she be but his doxy and not his wife
We'll filch her of him.

SECOND TIPPLER

Ay, he shall have a taste of the knife,
For he is but a foul, ill-favored lout,
But the wench is sweet flesh past all doubt.
Be she his doxy, I know where this night I shall lie.
Will aid me?

FIRST TIPPLER

In the throat, yea, that will I.
Foot to foot we will stand fast as we may. —
God a mercy, toper!

MOONEN

Pot-mates, come drink, I pray.

SECOND TIPPLER

Nay, toper, we drink of the same tun.
But may we sit you beside?

MOONEN

Yea, surely, that were well done.
Good fellowship is to me nothing loath.

FIRST TIPPLER

By your good leave, whence come ye both?

MOONEN

From Bolduc and beyond be we.

EMMA

Dear Moonen, were it not geometry
If perchance I could surely scan
How many drops of wine there be in a can?

33

MOONEN

Yea, love, and have ye the trick of that still?
I taught it you but yesterday.

EMMA

To forget it were ill.
Logic ye after taught me well and fair:
I hold it all fast in mind.

FIRST TIPPLER

Toper, what saith your wife there?
Can she soothly reckon to a jot
How many drops of wine be in this pot?
Of stranger thing I have never heard write.

MOONEN

She will do yet stranger in your sight.
Her like ye have never met withall;
The seven arts she hath mastered all;
Ars metric and geometry,
Logic, grammar, astronomy,
Music, and rhetoric, of ancientest repute.
With the stoutest clerk she dare dispute
In the schools of Paris or Louvain.

SECOND TIPPLER

Good toper, under your leave we were fain
See or hear some of her art.

FIRST TIPPLER

Yea, surely, and I pledge two stoups of wine for my part,
And, by cog's ribs, if any scant her in her tale
We will shed our blood for you without fail,
In any mischief that may you befall.

MOONEN

That merry ballat, as ye may call,
Wherewith our last noonday in Highstreet ye amused,
Do ye tell o'er for these folk.

EMMA

          I pray you hold me excused.
In rhetoric I be but a dull wight,
Allbe I would fain go to it with my might,
The circle of the seven arts to fulfill.
Rhetoric is not to be learned by skill;
'Tis an art that cometh of itself solely.
The other arts, if a man giveth himself thereto wholly,
These be to be learned and eke taught.

But rhetoric is to be praised beyond aught.
'Tis a gift of the Holy Ghost's bestowing,
Though there be rude folk of such small knowing
That they reject it. 'Tis great dole
To them who love it.

SECOND TOPER

                          Ay, good soul,
Must we use so much argument?

FIRST TOPER

Say us somewhat, we were well content
With what ye can, and out of good will
I will eke say somewhat.

EMMA

                       Now, hold ye still,
For rhetoric asketh good understanding;
And after my best cunning I will sing.

             ———

O rhetoric, sweet theoric and comfortable,
I lament with dreariment that men thee hate;
Unto the heart that loves thine art 'tis lamentable.

Cry on them fy! who thee not cultivate
Or thy first finder's fame abate!
Lewd and without shame are they.
Them I despise who do after this rate;
And to the wise 'tis grief to hear this say:
Through folly falls poesy to decay.

„Poesy hath praise": an ancient saying;
But weighing it, its mettle is but base:
Put case, a poet true art essaying
The braying of the unlettered race
Will chase him straightway forth from place,
Nor grace nor gear shall him repay.
But they some bold Tom Piper will agrace
Alway. Wherefore none may gainsay:
Through folly falls poesy to decay.

Fy ye blind and clumsy wits,
Poesy ye should strive to understand, and
Love it rightly, as befits.
Let it in honor on every hand stand;
By poesy only is a land grand.
Praise to them who own its sway!

Fy on the foolish who would have it out of hand
Wherefore yet once more I say :   [bann'd!
Through folly falls poesy to decay.

Prince, to poesy I will set my mind
And to its doctrine be faithfully inclined,
For it may be come at none other way.
But to the crafty seemeth it ever unkind
That the foolish be to poesy blind.

To hear this goodly ballat great press of folk gather-
ed and Moonen beholding this did after his hellish
kind and stirred among them such strife that one
among the folk was stabbed to death. And he who did
this had his head smote off. Thus Emma and Moonen
lived at Antwerp at the sign of the "Golden Tree" in
the market, where daily of his contriving were many
murders and slayings together with every sort of
wickedness. In the which he greatly rejoiced, saying
with himself thus :

What prodigy can I do?
Hell, I hope, will lend its aid thereto,
And get of it fair gain.

If but a little longer I may here reign,
Hell-mouth will be filled till it split.
'Twere a pity this good inn to quit,
For all who live in riot and wantonness
And win a profit of very idleness,
Gamblers, fighters, daughters of the game,
Bawds and all they who use the same,
Of these there be here a goodly retinue,
And 'tis of them my profit doth accrue.
Wherefore in this house as for this time I will lie.
Now will I go ask of mine host in hie
At what cost we twain lodge here.
If I do stay, I will have good cheer
And all things wholly to my pay.
Betide what betide I will as I may
Keep mischief stirring here and there.
Within a year I would see a hundred stabbed, I swear,
So that Lucifer shall not lack company in Hell.
As a doctor of physic I will disguise me well.
Good Doctor Gallipot shall not want for renown.
I shall know where to find hidden treasure in every
This will spread my fame over all.   [town.

And whatsoever among folk may befall
It will be known to me just as it was.
More than a thousand shall run after me ere there pass
A month, my practice will be so sly.
So I will get treasure with the which none can vie.
My love Emma will eke love me the bet.
An if the Highest doth me no let,
Ere a year more than a thousand souls I shall have
If He otherwise wills, then my baking is done. [won;

¶ How Emma doth a little lament her sinful life.

Emma thus dwelling in Antwerp and being ware of
the evil of her life, since for her sake marvelous much
wickedness was daily done of Moonen's contriving,
said with herself thus:

O memory and wit, took ye but thought
Upon the life that now I lead,
It would appear a thing of naught.
The brightness of Heaven ye have left and sought
The path of Hell, that is foul indeed.
Wellnigh each day doth some wight bleed
Or come even to his death for my sake.

And I wot well that Moonen doth this mischief breed.
He is not of the best, I undertake;
Though he saith little I may not him mistake:
He is a fiend or but little more.
O aunt, mine aunt, the foul words that ye spake
Will make of me a damned whore,
For whom God holds no grace in store.
Oh, woe is me and wellaway!
For any returning I bewandered too wide.
Mary I was wont to serve each day
With prayers or what else to her pay;
Now my devotions be wholly laid aside.
And eke he will me roundly chide
If I do cross myself, whereof he is not fain;
Whereby it is right easily descried
That he is evil, who crossing doth disdain.
How shall I repent? Alas, 'tis plain
That I be stept whither is no retreating.
Hola, yonder I have spied twain
To whom I yesterday did grant a merry meeting.
I must go forth and give them pleasant greeting.

After this she sat her down to drink with her pot-

41

mates, among the which Moonen so wrought that again one of them met his death. And he who did it was led of Moonen beyond the city walls where at the devil's prompting he slew yet another, in the hope, as Moonen had told, that he should thus possess him of great store of money; whereat Moonen rejoiced exceedingly saying:

Now by Lucifer's subtlest engine in Hell,
These silly folk I befool them well.
One to another doth tell that I am my Lord So and so.
All that aileth the people I fully know,
Wherefore after me doth go great press of folk.
I give them counsel as good as ever was spoke;
Then I round it in the ear of many a goodwife
How they may plague their husbands out of their life.
Whereon the goodman getteth such gobbets to his meat
That ere eight days he is snug in his winding sheet.
This merry cheat I have more than once played
And thereof Lucifer, I ween, is not evil apaid.
630 Likewise I take my good pleasure
In getting folk to seek out hidden treasure.
Thereby one got his bane but yesterday.

I told him where treasure had been hid away
Under the stay which did his stable found:
I said an he would delve deep in the ground
He would find many a pound of good red gold.
The fool straightway did as I told,
But when he had wholly digged away
The pillar's foundation which was the stay
That held the stable firm in place,
Down it fell from top to base
And good my nuncle was buried under.
I shall perform still greater wonder
If from above I may have leave.
Men shall me for a god receive;
And Hellwards they shall pack in troops.

After Emma and Moonen had lived wellnigh six year
in Antwerp at the sign of the "Golden Tree", where
marvelous much wickedness was done of them, it fell
out that Emma was minded once more to see her eme
and likewise her friends in the land of Guelders, and
she prayed Moonen that he should thereto consent
and fellow her on the journey thither, whereon he
spake thus :

Emma, to your prayer I would not say no.
Ye say your friends ye would liefly see?

EMMA

Yea, that I would, if ye grant it so.

MOONEN

To your prayer, my love, I would not say no.

EMMA

Mine aunt at Nimmegen, mine eme at Venlo;
Sin I saw them be passed years four and three.

MOONEN

Wherefore to your prayer I will not say no.
And these your friends ye shall straightway see.

EMMA

They know not what hath befallen me
Nor where I be, no more than if earth had me swal-
Ever mine eme with love hath me followed;   [lowed.
I wot full many a tear he hath wept.

MOONEN

The old shave-crown's prayers me oft have kept
When I was minded to rend her limb and lith.

Ere now I had broken her neck, but therewith
The old man's prayers to the lady in white
Have stopped me quite; wherefore, despite
My will, not yet is she utterly caught.

EMMA

What say ye, Moonen?

MOONEN

Nought, dear, nought.

I give you leave, as ye require,
To see the friends to whom is your desire.
Go pay the reckoning with mine host of the Tree
And on the morrow thine eme we shall go see
Or thine other friends, as ye shall request.
To this I am prest.

EMMA

Then straight am I dress'd
To ask how it stands in our account
And pay it all wholly.

MOONEN

So do, and the amount
See that ye pay without question of the odd doit. —

I shall get no loss from this exploit,
'Tis no harm to visit her eme, the priest.
If I could catch him bare-breeched, at the least,
And so have him wholly at my desire,
I would shortly break the old shave-poll's swire.
Were he away, the lass were mine without fail.
But my purpose is wholly without avail,
Save only the Omnipotent
Giveth thereto his full consent.

¶ How Emma and Moonen journeyed to Nimmegen.

Thus Emma and Moonen journeyed to Nimmegen,
where they be come on Procession Day, whereat
Emma rejoiced exceedingly. And Moonen to her
spake thus:

Now, Emma, even as ye of me prayed,
Hither our journey we have made
To Nimmegen; and 'tis Procession Day.
Here your aunt had her dwelling, as ye say.
Will ye go see her?

EMMA

Yea, so much, mayhap;
But for lodging I would not ask her, nor for a scrap
To eat nor yet a drop to drink;
Thereof I would not think, lest o'er me she skink
The flood of her reproach, and entreat me once more
Even so shamelessly as she hath done yore.
'Twas the foul and wicked words she spake
Made me to these ill courses take,
The which I still am in, alas!

MOONEN

I bethink me, my love and solace,
That to go thither will little bestead.
Know your aunt is three years dead.

EMMA

What say ye, dead?

MOONEN

Yea, it is so.

EMMA

How know ye that?

MOONEN

Enough, I know.

EMMA

. . . . . . This is not light to bear.

MOONEN

'Tis e'en so.

EMMA

Stay, what do they there?
Let us go look ere from hence we depart.
See what a press of people forth doth start.
Is it aught to see? Haste ye and enquire amain.

MOONEN

Nay, love, they will play somewhat on the pageant-
[wain.

EMMA

That do they every year on this day,
And as I mind, "Maskeroon" is the play.
Its goodly excellence is not lightly to be told,
Mine eme each year failed not it to behold.
Ah, Moonen, let us hear it.

MOONEN

'Tis silly gabbling.
Wherefore would ye give ear to such brabbling?
Bah, go we to the roast meat and the wine.

48

EMMA

Ah, Moonen, it was wont to be so brave and fine.
I have heard mine eme say that for its teaching
The play was better than many a preaching.
And in these plays oft times good ensamples there be.
Ah, love, if ye would thereto agree
I would fain see it.

MOONEN

          To consent I am not glad. —
By Lucifer's rump, I am sore adrad
Lest in the play she behold some virtuous condition
Whereof haply she may catch contrition.
By Lucifer, then were my high designs brought low.

EMMA

Ay, Moonen, let me hear it.

MOONEN

          Well, see that ye be not slow
To come when I call, else will my wrath be great.

Emma besought Moonen so hardly that she might
hear the play that he thereto consented, though sorely

against his will as ye have heard. And the play began thus;

MASKEROON

Brr! hierio! I, Maskeroon, Lucifer's advocate,
Make my appeal before the assize
Of Him called of men Most High and All Wise,
Because He showeth to the vile human race
More of His pity and of His grace
Than to us poor spirits, damned perpetually.
If all the sins that in the world there be
Were wholly done by one sole man
And then in heartfelt earnest he began
To feel remorse, straight he to grace hath won.
And we poor spirits, who have nought misdone,
Save for one brief presumptuous thought,
We be to the abyss down brought,
Hopeless in everlasting pain.
I, Lucifer's procurator, ask again
The God of mercy wherefor of His grace
Comes less to us than to the race
Of men who daily sin on every side.

GOD

My mercy is to none denied
Who will repent him ere he die
And in season confess that I
Am God of justice and mildheartedness.
But they that grow hard in wickedness
And will not truly them repent
With Lucifer in the pit they shall be shent,
Where is wailing and hand-wringing.

MASKEROON

Thy justice fails in many a thing,
Though Thou art a just God called in every land and
In Abraham's, in Moses', and in Davids' time   [clime.
Men might Thee indeed the just name,
But then didst Thou men blame and eke shame
And punish them for uncleanness of thought.
Nowadays though a child were with his mother naught,
Or spurned his father underfoot and him smote,
Yea, though one should thrust down his brother's throat
All the evil that in the world is brewed,
And then but repented him in mood,
Straightway to him is thine abundant grace supplied.

51

GOD

Wherefore was it I the death died
Shamefully upon the cross of tree,
Were it not that man, whether young or old he be,
Might get him mercy at the hands of my Father?

MASKEROON

Wherefore shouldst Thou be wroth the rather,
In as much as Thou, naked and in vain,
Didst in Thy shameful death suffer such pain,
That mankind should be clean of sin;
Despite the which they do harden themselves in
Wickedness so unseemly and fell
That uneath may one it reckon and tell,
And but to think on maketh the mind distraught.
Such things as under the old law were not thought
Men do now boldly perform them as soon.

GOD

Therein thou liest not, Maskeroon:
The people be indeed so hard grown in sin
That, if some amendment doth not shortly begin,
My sharp sword of justice I will presently send,

Which shall cut off all them that do offend,
And eke My plagues, which are not light to endure.

OUR LADY

My child, if mankind with plagues Thou wouldst cure
It were to me pure sorrow. Let Thy wrath be staid.
Let there for man still a respite be made;
Send Thou him first a sign and a token,
Even as erewhile Thou hast unto him spoken:
Earthquakes, twin suns, or a hairy star,
That by these portents he may know how far
Thou art stepped beyond the measure of Thy wrath.
Thus peradventure man will leave the path
Of sin, lest he be worse plagued to his cost.

GOD

Nay, Mother, that were but labor lost;
I have full oft My portents shown,
Whereby My wrath they might well have known;
Pestilence, war, and season of dearth,
The which should have brought repentance upon earth
For the sins which wrong My divinity.
But the worse they are plagued the worse they be,

53

Not thinking of wailful death for ever and aye.
'Tis all: "what care I? At the last a prayer I will say
And the merciful God will save me from harm."

Emma hearkening to this play bethought her of her
sinful life with sad heart, with herself saying:

Lord God, how doth my blood grow warm
At the words I hear spoke on yon pageant-wain.
These be reasons and arguments so plain
That pure contrition I do begin to know.

MOONEN

Well, must we stand here forever? What say ye, ho!
Wherefore to hear this brabbling be ye fain?
Let us be gone, love.

EMMA

                                    Nay, it is lost pain
Thus to call and hale and tug at me in this way.
Even so long as lasteth the play
To make me budge a step nought will avail.
'Tis better than a sermon.

54

MOONEN

Help, Lucifer's tail !

I am in despair that here she should stay,
Lest to repentance she catch the nearest way
With the foolish blether to the which she giveth heed.
I will bide awhile, but if she cometh not erelong with
'Twill be my fists shall furnish arguments.   [speed

MASKEROON

O ruler of the heavens and the elements,
God that in justice sittest enthroned,
If but to Lucifer and the infernal synod were loaned
Thy will and power, then could we
Chastise mankind all utterly
Until from sinning they shall cease.
Thus only canst Thou win surcease
And they release, from the evils they do in Thy
Thy hand of justice must them smite   [despight.
If Thou wouldst make Thee known of men.

GOD

Maskeroon, it may not be over long till then
And I give thee leave to plague mankind,

For to good they will not be inclined
Or ere their stubborn necks I bend.

OUR LADY

O son, men will yet their evil ways amend.
Bethink Thee ere too swift Thy hand hath struck.
Bethink Thee on the breasts that gave Thee suck,
Bethink Thee on the bosom that did Thee enfold,
Bethink Thee on the passion Thou hast tholed,
Bethink Thee of the blood-offering Thou didst make.
Was it not all done for man his sake
That to Thy Father's mercy he might win?
Thyself hast said that if a man should sin
In his sole self of sins each one
That ever upon earth were done
And heartily on Thee for mercy cried,
Thine arms to him would open wide.
This is Thy word as man well wot.

GOD

Lady Mother, I have spoken, and repent Me not,
But I say again that if a man commit
All the sins whereto he could bethink him in his wit,

If he confess and repent he shall be of the chosen
For liefer than one soul should go astray [straightway;
I would suffer all the pain twice o'er
Which the Jews did unto Me in days of yore.
O man, this it behooveth thee to know.

―――――

The longer Emma hearkened to this play, even the
more she bethought of her sins, saying thus:

Now do my tears begin to flow
And course adown my cheeks like rain.
Ah, to what contrition I do now attain
At hearkening to these words; O Lord of Lords,
Were it possible that should I turn me towards
Thy mercy, I might have of it some part?
Ere now contrition hath visited not my heart.
Were it possible? Alas, I fear me nay.
I be wandered too far out of the way,
Not letting reason be of my will the guide.
Open, O Earth, swallow me and hide,
For I am not worthy to tread on thee in any wise.

57

MOONEN

Help Modicack, how the flames start from mine eyes;
The lass hath got a crop full of contrition.

. . . .

To some merry part of the town haste we
And there crush a cup of wine.

EMMA

Nay, let be,

Foul fiend, be gone without any tarrying!
Woe's me, that ever I did such a thing
As summon you, God's mercy all forgot.
Ah, ah! repentance within me doth burn so hot
It will consume my heart. Alas, I swound!
My strength hath left me.

MOONEN

Lucifer's lights, liver and spleen confound!
Now may I sputter flames and howl;
Now runneth all my fair to foul;
And they who prowl in Hell will give me small acclaim.
Rise up in all the devils' name
Or with hosen and shoon into the jakes ye go.

EMMA

O Lord, have mercy upon me!

MOONEN

Yea, stands it so?

Now I perceive remorse in her doth gnaw.
Up into the clouds I will her draw
And towering high down hurl her with might and with
If she to herself do come again,   [main;
The whelp may think her luck is fair. —
Here, here, ye go with me aloft in the air.

After these words hath Moonen the devil caught up
Emma in the air higher than is any house or church,
the which her uncle and all the people beheld, wonder-
ing exceedingly and not knowing what it might mean.

¶ How Moonen cast down Emma from on high and
how she was discovered to her uncle.

When Moonen the devil had caught up Emma high
above all the houses, he cast her down from above
into the street as he was minded to break her neck,
whereat the people were sore adrad. And Sir Gysbrecht, her eme, who hearkened also to the play,
marveled what it meant and who it might be that fell

59

from so great height, saying and asking of them that
stood by thus:

Her luck is good if her neck be not broke in twain.
My heart feeleth unutterable pain
To look on one in such array.
Know ye her not? Who is the woman, I pray?

A BURGHER

I would fain see if I know her, without a doubt,
But there be such press of folk hereabout
That I may nowise come her to.
Follow me close, and ye shall see what I will do.
He is a fool says I am not stout to make them give
See ye, sir, the poor lady lieth in a swound,   [ground.
She be gone out of herself.

THE UNCLE

                        It is small wonder so.
Help, all the blood of my body from top to toe
Be crept from me forth, as I deem.
The tears do from mine eyes stream;
My veins be dead and my color turned into pale;

Never thus have I felt my strength fail.
Ah friend, have a care of me, I you beseech.

THE BURGHER

Stay sir, what aileth you, as by your speech?
Ye be changed as if ye were but dead.

THE UNCLE

I would well that were my fate instead.
O Atropos, grant me of my life release!

THE BURGHER

Wherefore do ye thus?

THE UNCLE

Oh, it is my niece,
For the which my heart is fulfilled of sorrow.
For her have I searched this seven year on even
[and on morrow.
Now lieth she here with her neck broken in twain.
O earth, open and swallow me amain;
Here I would no longer tarry.

THE BURGHER

Be ye sure 'tis she?

THE UNCLE

        Should I not know her, marry?
Or mean ye that in my wit I fail?

MOONEN

Fire and brimstone, lightning and hail!
I befoul my tail out of pure ire;
But to a remedy I am none the nigher.
Yonder is her uncle; I am to cook this but will ye tell
I had broken her neck long ere now,   [me how?
But that the prayers of this holy priest
To make hard my way have not ceased.
An I might I would carry him straight to Lucifer.

THE BURGHER

Look, sir, I do see her somewhat stir.

THE UNCLE

Stir! That were the boot of all my bale.
'Tis true, she doth stir sikerly.

EMMA

        Alas, what doth to me ail?
Where have I been, and be now in what place?
O Lord, stand I in Thy grace

That to Thy mercy I may come?
Yea, but Thy care had kept me from
The fiend, O Lord omnipotent,
In lasting torment I were shent,
Thrust soul and body beyond the reach
And scope of the Lord's realm.

THE UNCLE

Since ye have speech,
Mary, my niece, then speak to me,
Who so many sighs for thee
Have sighed and many a moan have made,
Nor ever my questionings have staid;
And now I find you in this press, as it doth seem
In sorry plight.

EMMA

Ah, is it ye, mine eme?
Ah, would God I were in that case
Even now as then I was
When I last saw you ere my long journey was begun.
Ah, when my course of life I overrun
I fear me I am damned for aye.

THE UNCLE

Niece, ye err, I trow,

For none is lost who will not yield him so.

How should ye be damned? That were pity indeed.

How came ye hither? I would fain know with speed;

And ye were so high in air but now.

I prithee tell me thereof, if ye would allow.

Never saw I any so high, by my troth.

EMMA

Mine eme, I be alas full loath

To reckon up the tale of my aventures.

I gave me over wholly to the devil's lures,

And after I have gone about with him for wellnigh

[seven year.

I may not lightly set it all clear, but thus briefly ye

shall hear

Whither our way of life hath us took.

One could well thereof write a book.

There is none evil with mine which may compare;

And at the end of all this strange fare

I am come hither in land my friends to behold.

And even now as this way we strolled

We saw them in the market-place here
Playing the play of Maskeroon, to the which I gave ear.
At every word which I there heard
I caught such a contrition that it stirred
Him to wrath that stood by me and he flew,
Even as ye saw, high with me into air.

THE UNCLE

Alas and harru!

How, niece, was it the fiend that was with you here?

EMMA

Yea, eme, and 'tis now well nigh seven year
Since I yielded me to do his will and went
A wandering with him.

THE UNCLE

Help, God omnipotent!

Hearing this maketh me all aghast.
We must drive this fiend from you at the last,
If God's kingdom ye would come to.

MOONEN

Ay, shave-crown, that may ye not do;
Ye may not me from her divide.

If it pleased me I would carry her hair and hide
Where is sulphur and pitch a plenty at the least.

THE UNCLE

Would ye, foul fiend?

MOONEN

        Yea, that I would, horson priest.
She is mine, she hath yielded herself all wholly,
And renounced the Most High, and held with me,
Wherefore in the furnace of hell she must burn.
And, horson, would ye her from me turn?
I will strike you down all plat.

THE UNCLE

Foul fiend, I will let you of that.
Here in my breviary there stand
Eight or ten lines writ in a fair nand
Which will make you grin all otherwise.

MOONEN

Ah! ah! my fell of bristles doth rise
At the words he readeth; I know nor what to do nor
By Modicack, if she should scape me now   [how.
I shall be whipped with burning lash!

Yea, in rage my teeth I gnash,
And blow sparks from mouth and ears.
Now in me full plain appears
That if the Lord's wrath we arouse in aught,
All we spirits may do is less than nought.
I fear me with this soul I need no longer tarry.

THE UNCLE

Go we, niece Mary, and I will you carry
To the deacon's and there make up a fire.
Methinks your limbs be broke, for higher
He flew with you than one can think and then
Ye must be sore hurt.   [let fall,

EMMA

                              I count it nought at all
This pain, mine eme; though remedy be none.
More by ten thousand times I would not shun
Than all that pens could write for anything,
If only to me God's mercy would cling.
I care not what befalls if but one day
Comfort and mercy may be mine.

THE UNCLE

                              Keep you in that way,
I promise you God's kingdom to your cure.
We read alday in the blessed Scripture
That him who on God's mercy would him cast
Nought so avails as repentance at the last.

After this Sir Gysbrecht is gone with his niece to all
the most learned priests in the town of Nimmegen,
but none of them, howsoever learned or expert or
holy or devout, when they heard her story, durst undertake to absolve her or to prescribe to her penance
for her sins, the which were fearful and against kind,
whereat both they were sore downcast.

¶ How Sir Gysbrecht journeyed to Cologne with
his niece.

The next day at early morn Sir Gysbrecht made pre-
parations as if he would celebrate mass taking the
precious holy sacrament in his hand and set out with
Emma his niece on the way to Cologne. And Moonen the devil followed them from afar but he dare

not approach nigh nor draw near to Emma in any wise on account of the power of the holy sacrament. Nevertheless he threw sometimes the half of an oak tree or another from above at them, minded to break both their necks, but our Lord would not allow it for she used daily to read a prayer in honor of our Blessed Lady. Thus they traveled so long and much that they came to Cologne where she confessed to the Bishop. But there no man knew what counsel to give her for her sin was so against kind and great that the Bishop had not power to absolve her.

❡ How Emmaand her Unclejourneyed to Rome and how Emma confessed her to the Pope.

After this Emma and her eme departed them from the Bishop and leaving Cologne journeyed to Rome, where they be come after much travail and journey-ing. And Emma has made confession to the Pope with weeping eyes, saying:

O God's vice-gerent, yea, God on earth, as we be told,
A sinner worse than I earth doth not hold;
Shut out from the bar of Heaven I be.

THE POPE

Wherefore, my child?

EMMA

The devil's amie
I have been yea more than seven year
And with him have wandered far or near
Even at our will, and know ye for truth
Whatso man and wife do we have done in sooth.
Now say ye not that to fear me I do well?

THE POPE

What, child, and was it the fiend out of hell?
And wist ye that, when ye together went,
The fiend he was?

EMMA

Yea, father reverent.

THE POPE

How could ye with the fiend have ado
If ye wist 'twas he?

EMMA

Father, 'twas merry days for us two,
And the broad gold and all the rich fare

The which he gave me, be ye well ware
'Twas these tempted me, wherefore I am now shamed.
There was nought in the whole world that I named
He did not give it me straight even as I willed.
But this with the sorrow whereof I now most am filled,
And the which hath my heart cleft clean in twain,
'Tis that so many folk were slain
Whithersoever we be come in our way.
More than two hundred, reverend father, I say,
Be for my sake miserably dead,
One time or another.

THE POPE

Almighty Godhead!
For such misdeeds ye may well live in sorrow.

EMMA

O father, if it may be, be to me borrow
And give me penance or ere we part,
I reck not how heavy.

THE POPE

I scarce have heart
To tent so deep into the mercy of the Lord.

71

What, that ye should with the fiend be at accord!
Such crimes in confession I have not heard tell!
And furthermore by your wiles ye have sent pell-mell
So many the way their life they should lose!
I may scarce know what penance to choose
Heavy enough for such mortal sin.
To dwell with the fiend was but a bestial life to be in.
O Godhead, whereof doth not begin or end the grace,
Wilt Thou guide me as in this case,
Beneath the which my wit doth bow and bend!
O Judge enthroned in justice, do Thou send
Thine inspiration from on high!
Hola, my course I clear descry;
Me were full loath that damned ye be.
The priest was with you, summon hither to me.
Your penance ye shall hear without all doubt.

EMMA

Where be ye, eme?

THE UNCLE

I stand here without,
And full of care till it doth appear
How it shall go with her.

THE POPE

Now ye my judgment hear:
It were a thing right pitiful to see
That any should be damned, if cure there be,
Nor doth God unmoved behold such things.
See, here be three iron rings;
The greatest ye shall her neck lock round,
The other two, without sigh or sound,
Lock on her arms, both fast and strong.
And let her bear them how so long
It be that they wear away and fall.
1080 Then shall her sins be forgiven all.
Nor till then shall she be of them quit.

THE UNCLE

'Twill be full long, as to my wit,
Ere of themselves they fall to ground,
For they be of weight so many a pound
That in an hundred year they will wear never
A farthing thickness.

THE POPE

Yet may she so persever
Heartily in a state of penitence

73

That the rings will of themselves fall hence
From neck and arms and leave them bare.
But see ye lock them fast.

THE UNCLE

Father, I swear
They shall be locked so stout and stark,
If they come off 'twill be God's mark.
O priest and clerk above each earthly state,
With your good favor we will take our leave straight,
And go again our gate back to the land
Whence we be come.

THE POPE

May He whose hand
Dispenseth mercy soften your affliction.

EMMA

Adieu, holy Father.

THE POPE

Daughter, go in God's protection,
And keep ye wholly in penitence,
For above with the Highest Excellence

Is pure penitence held more dear
Than ought that we may read or hear.

Thus hath Emma received her penance from the
Pope. And her eme straightway let make the rings
so fast about her neck and arms that in her lifedays
they might not be done off but by the will and the
miracle of our dear Lord.

❡ How Emma journeyed from Rome and how she
became a nun at the cloister of Converted Sinners at
Maestricht.

Whenas Emma hath put on the rings like as ye have
heard she departed her with her eme from Rome the
city and they two journeyed so long until they were
come to Maestricht where Emma was holpen of her
uncle to be a nun in the cloister of the Converted
Sinners. And after he had thereto holpen her he took
his leave of her and journeyed to his own country
where he lived yet twenty-four year after he had
holpen his niece to come into the cloister, the which
he visited each year so long as he lived.

❡ How the angel of God did off the rings from Emma's neck and hands.

Emma dwelling in the aforesaid cloister lived so holily and did such strong penance that the merciful Christ forgave her utterly her sins, sending his angel to her where she lay and slept, the which did off the rings, whereat Emma rejoiced greatly, saying:

Long nights are little to him lief
Who lieth sorrowful of heart;
His sleep is great unrest or greater grief,
With fearsome dreams and other such mischief.
Even thus I now feel sorrow's smart.
Who will the meaning to me impart
Of this my dream wherein I lay?
Meseemed from hell-pit I did start
And heavenwards was borne away.
There many white doves I met in the way,
The which my bonds struck with their wings.
O merciful God, what see I? Stay!
To Thine high grace have I won for aye?
Ah yea, 'tis true; there be my rings

Beside me lying. King of kings,
What cure art Thou for all misease!
No thanks suffice Thee for to please
In any stound.
O man, in whom all sin is found,
Hereby may ye ensample take;
And to His worth that knows no bound
Let everlasting laud and praise resound,
Even such as your faint voice may wake:
Praise ye the Lord in His temple for the Lord His sake.

EPILOGUE

Even thus, O ye whom God loves well,
In days of yore these things befell
All truly, though some hold it for a fable.
But go ye to Maestricht, an ye be able,
And in the Converted Sinners shall ye see
The grave of Emma, and there all three
The rings be hung above her grave.
Thereunto stands writ in goodly stave
Her way of life and her penance
And how and when all this did chance.